Tearing Petals of Beauty

Poems and Paintings

by

Bailey C. Weber

To order additional copies of this book, contact:
Xlibris
844-714-8691
www.Xlibris.com
Orders@Xlibris.com

ISBN:	Softcover	978-1-6698-1250-0
	Hardcover	978-1-6698-1251-7
	EBook	978-1-6698-1249-4
Library of Congress Control Number:		2022902890

Print information available on the last page

Rev. date: 02/18/2022

SECTION ONE

Personal Favorites

March 6

With sorrowful grief, this is my silence
Look what was started—art kills the artist
The man's heart is filled with hidden violence
The anger of the man I gladly kissed
Walk through the garden gate smelling roses
Pulling up weeds to sustain beauty's air
Beneath the fragrant flowers, death poses
Love slowly seeing, but no one will stare
Watering my happiness, I forget
Consumed by beauty and never cower
Crying with trying tears, the ground buds hit
Rotting with the perfume of the flower
Loving art, distracted by my eye's view
Torn by thorns and terror, rose petals blew

The Flower Petals Blush

Facing boredom, looking it in the eye
I stare at the anger inside of me
The inner peace within you is a lie
A lie that your mouth cannot ever see
You never can be content with the weeds
The weeds that overtake the flower field
You cannot love all and beauty will bleed
My emotions inside I tried to yield
As I show you the way to the flowers
My heart is never within you, not now
Consuming your mind's heat, the sun cowers
Black and white to listen you won't allow
Show the colors you could not ever touch
Breathing deeply, the flower petals blush

Longing Lavender

Most cannot think for their own selves ever
Sniffing the lavender, I can't tell them
Manipulating words, I am clever
Was this sorrowful shrub for you or him?
I walk by him smelling like sweet perfume
Tell it like it is; don't scream lies at me
It is abnormal to safely assume
Promise love's opportunity to be
Strolling through flowery herbs, adventure starts
In warm summer, my wise heart remains pure
With time's test, true devotion never parts
Natural remedy's fragrance will cure
Their content satisfaction is waiting
In love's happiness, senses are mating

Internal Monarch

You tell me I leave a void with despair
Are you in there? Don't you remember me?
Decorating wings, a beautiful pair
Ugly caterpillar, I used to be
I gave you hope when none was to be found
Do you think hope void of any a lie?
Because golden yellow a lovely sound
And beauty has not a reason to cry
I have a summer shadow within me
Happy but dark, and I show you the truth
You say truth and despair the same in me
But golden yellow is never uncouth
You misunderstand the beauty in me
Representing atrocity, are we?

Balance for the Dainty Daisy

If a flower I were to be, I would
Find myself then as a dainty daisy
Pretend indifference, I wish I but could
The love within you is never lazy
Give me a piece of your heart, of your soul
Give me a piece of your hand that I hold
Whatever I take becomes a deep hole
Dainty daisy with an elegant scold
Yellow surrounded—tiny white petals
As many alterations as can be
This dainty daisy controls and meddles
Noticing you, I forget about me
Because intense, spirited love for you
Is within me and whimsy within you

Running Up the Mountains in the Horizon

I'm an Appalachian woman at heart
Love and hate mountains at the horizon
With disappointment, loud lectures will start
Always on the trail in the woods I run
Cherokee rose bush along the dirt path
Waterfalls flow over slippery rocks
Prefer flowers because they have no wrath
The water talks the talk and walks the walk
Yet I cannot bring myself near to it
So I run back to the Cherokee rose
And a loss for words, a wonder for wit
Because the flower thinks of us as foes
The thorns tear my flesh, and I remember
The woods in the mountains in September

Some Flowers I Love

When I die, I do not want a casket
I wish for the worms to eat my decay
Meditate in my black room, rot and sit
Be fertilized by me the flowers may
For the begonia and black-eyed- Susan
For sunflowers and daisies and bluebells
And every pretty flower that has been
Any luscious petal a story tells
As it is written, so it shall be done
I hate being useless, and I hate pain
Remedy the former, latter is gone
Flowers in the earth a colorful stain
Clematis, iris, lilac, hydrangea
Lily, lavender, and echinacea

SECTION TWO

Love Poems

Evangeline Sweet

His voice failed, and the song faded away

Lovers have not unconditional love

The music of the moment may not stay

But one must sing to the ginkgo above

Struggling with her heart, Evangeline sweet

Past happiness he never overcame

Follow the ginkgo's path and tread your feet

Loving his life, Evangeline her name

He was the song she sang, touching his hair

Gentle kisses blessing, the ginkgo leads

Her voice weak and smooth, her love strong and fair

Musical spirit, love everyone needs

And Evangeline pleads to the ginkgo

With a gift of love, loud the song shall grow

Honeysuckle and Clematis

Twining toward each other, they tangle
Honeysuckle and clematis in love
Twining toward each other, they tangle
They grow together in the bonds of love
Beautiful in their purple and pink heart
Complement each other, they always feel
Their soulful love only petals apart
Euphoric allure bestirs, always feel
Down on his knees, he looks into my face
I cannot help but to adore his love
Saying "yes" with my teardrops on my face
To the soft petals pretty in their love
He feels his looks of love returned by me
Honeysuckle and clematis to be

Message to the World

Hatred manages to profane my speech

I ask myself why I am so angry

Lyrics of beauty, my mind cannot reach

Within my loving heart, strife is to be

The hydrangea bush chose sorrow and shade

Forget to find beauty in the ugly

The vibrant colors shall not ever fade

Forgiveness, always be found within me

The blue of the flower turns to purple

There is an amethyst within the dirt

Finding no fault, pink forms from the purple

Still growing in shade, a moonstone will flirt

Love can be found wherever one shall look

Singing to the earth, my voice never took

Por Amor

¿Adónde yo voy por mi corazón?
Like a trillium in the spring season
Hearing your eyes, I miss your voice's tone
Spring always to vanish without reason
I felt for you within a soft petal
My fingers destroy the flower's beauty
Crumpling to dust, I cry for the petal
First love will always forget its duty
Like a trillium flower within spring
Blooming everywhere, I finally see
To our second date, a kiss I shall bring
Trilliums forget about you and me
First love won't come back like a trillium
But final love becomes a trillium

Sisterly Cecilia and Lorelei

Sisters Cecilia and Lorelei

Loving separately but growing, they wave

Different flowers, but never say good-bye

Lorelei pretty; Cecilia brave

Cecilia radiant, strikes the sun

Lorelei lovely, calming anxious lakes

The water lily, aloof, is as one

The echinacea, furious it takes

Jealousy should have no expectation

Disappointment more echinacea breeds

The water lily tries for temptation

Lorelei, younger, eventually leads

Treated the same, but turning out different

And now, nature names wherever love went

Free, Not Trite

Showing me the truth, at least now I know
Peonies will fight among the roses
Clouding the eyes, beauty a moral foe
In poetry, reality poses
Peonies more elegant and less trite
Forgetting words, poetry not for me
Admiring flowers, colors pastel, light
Confusing me, sentences tangle, flee
Like loose petals in the heart's lovely wind
I will look for those of the peony
For the other lover, kisses will send
He desires to touch me, staring at me
His hand goes up my knee, and I consent
Within poems, peonies won't resent

Love in Moonlight

Make mine moonlight, poets say to the sky
Enlightening, give me understanding
Night awakening, dark my breath will sigh
Belle and Sebastian in love still standing
Forget about the stars and stare at me
And I cannot breathe when you look at me
Stars bright and beautiful, but never free
Conquering all is the moon within me
Belle and Sebastian poor without money
Have you ever spoken an honest word?
Angels above all are the stars to be
The evil concept of power absurd
Greedy and arrogant, the moon knows not
The night sky thinks of nothing and smokes pot

Strawberries

Strawberries, sweet and juicy, soft and ripe
In this world, there is love for everyone
I experiment as I find my type
Know always strawberries are never gone
And you will find the romantic fruit too
And you will have flirtatious looks on you
Nervous and shaky, but your heart rings true
Overcoming fears, you are proud of you
Love is so simple until it is not
Strawberries overly ripe, not just soft
Looking at another, your eye is caught
Regret in your mind, your strength has grown soft
But you remember the strawberries now
Your morals to rot you will not allow

A Heavy Dream

I have given up on everything now
My disappointments come from excitement
Depression in all of my nightmares now
At my anxieties, my brain will hint
It is like when you cannot sleep and you
Wake up in a cold sweat, a heavy dream
You do not know what I discuss, do you?
I say you dreamed about me in my dream
But that is an absolute living lie
And I cannot even remember you
An unknown face, so I cannot yet cry
But I reveal I still somehow love you
Love you in a simple, sweet, painful way
Painful as your memory will not stay

Sinking Louisiana

Starry-eyed Louisiana, you love
The starry-eyed will never be the same
Lost in the swamp, my heart must find its love
For the misfortune, you never to blame
And I cannot sleep until you hold me
And now I never can dream anymore
And you—you instantly need to find me
And realize cruelty's love forever more
Wish swampy chaos was a clear, calm stream
But live for Louisiana's romance
Remnants remaining, but different you seem
Mutilation's beauty hearts will enhance
You are lost in the swamp, and so am I
I forget you are a dream by-and-by

Vampires, Love, and Blood

For sweet blood, I am thirsty in the throat
A quaint, quirky heart will follow me now
To the mortal belle, love I would devote
Evil hinders; death's darkness I allow
Tender pain together: myself and you
My corruption and chaos cannot go
In agony: I'm sorry I hurt you
Finite life, relationships have sorrow
A genuine sincere apology
I become honest as you fade away
Screaming my lungs are forever to be
Nurturing for you to die anyway
Crying and tender, but my soul is feared
Love creating dehydration, I'm scared

Betray the Beliefs

In case you forget, I'm here to remind
You are the one who taught me to believe
Drawings impressive: your talent, I find
You are not an artist; deceits achieve
Manipulating emotions, you are
Trust betrays me when I draw in the dark
Shadows will shine if I sketch who you are
Losing my light, my soul sits in the dark
My mind standing by, body cannot sleep
I dream of color within the blackness
My heart awakes, the thought of you, I keep
All is impossible outside madness
Trapped in sanity, I miss touching you
Ideas talk silent when love proves true

Firefly Yells Yellow

Soft and mellow, lighting up lively love
My blazing fire scorched your feelings away
My bright yellow yells in the sky above
Wings flying fast, but beauty here to stay
You know I would gladly burn my dead heart
Yelling yellow becomes anger, then rage
And again, screaming silence will not part
Because freedom inside a deadly cage
Apologize: I know I should to you
Trap my emotions, yellow will escape
I forget about me when I help you
Looking within at my body's landscape
Yellow will glow in the black and the night
Blind the normal in the absence of light

Pale Purple Lilacs Bloom Again

You knew all along that it was not you
Look away from the pale purple lilacs
Mourning love's beauty, purple petals blew
Wilt away holding bouquets of lilacs
Emotions escape your heart early on
Dust remains, left: find fault with words and lips
I will leave you behind when I am gone
Thinking of me, a flower petal rips
And you regret when words wither within
You never could tell me what your mind thought
With love blossoming, lilacs bloom again
Winter blinding feelings; sight, summer brought
Spring always melts away our deadly hate
In hugging forgiveness, never be late!

Happy Summer Day

Beauty in the air, a warm breeze will blow
And sunshine is pouring down onto me
There are flowers surrounding the willow
They're getting pollinated by a bee
And the honeysuckle is so happy
To have attention from the hummingbird
And the maple tree is very sappy
And there's a pretty noise from the songbird
Underneath the willow: a lively pond
Duck heads underwater and swim peaceful
Of the happy summer day, I am fond
Of appreciation, my heart is full
Because there is always love I can see
And proposing, he is down on one knee

Protector of Children

Lost in the darkness, I'll find you somewhere
I won't stop searching until our embrace
Looking for shapes, in the blackness, I stare
In my memory's vision, see your face
Aspiring to find you, I am ablaze
Awaiting you somehow, I feel awry
Stepping, place my feet and follow my gaze
With desperation crazy by-and-by
Protector of children here within me
Righteous sadness someway reforms in you
Aloof interference a part of me
Because I do not think of change in you
Protector of children, a spirit here
And because of them, you are without fear

April Rain

The unforgiving feeling of doubt grows

Every season is filled with April rain

Dampness in your joints, tingling in your nose

Dry-rot with water droplets and disdain

Summer should be smiling, but instead frowns

Damp already a depressing spirit

And misery within the happy clowns

Happiness far away, yet you fear it

And I feel I do not belong with you

Don't you know it does not get easier?

Love and romance never found within you

The coldness blustering and breezier

Because musty and dry-rotting you are

Naked I am: I think tempted you are!

Waterfalls and Cataracts

A storm stirring mud somewhere deep inside
My eyes cloud over as memories shine
Mindful thunder and lightning I abide
Because his love will forever be mine
The waterfall's cataracts do reflect
A rainbow with the colors and the light
Waterfalls singing of cause and effect
Because remember love always as bright!
Pupils are grey, personality there
River dancing maidens with armpit stains
Here by the waterfall as he will stare
Enchantment! Me with my talent and brains
He chose me that day by the waterfall
Thinking of him, my tears forever fall

Gardenia and Gladiolus

I met you in my heart's flower garden

But we are worlds away, and I have fear

Gardenia and Gladiolus within

Thinking of you, my passion always clear

My petals travel the world to find you

Grow in experience, grow in wisdom

But my quest is to find you, to woo you

Flower garden in my heart a kingdom

And you will come, and you will be here too

And that is all I ever ask of you

I finally found the marvel of you

And righteously so, gape in love at you

And we are king and queen of the garden

Our beautiful blameless triumph within

Zinnia

Consistent affection will always last

Absent friends, and I always think of them

Losing you, but forgiveness in the past

I remember daily my love for him

A pious zinnia flower, he gave me

I saw my virtue reflected in it

And I reminded myself who to be

I look at the church pillars where I sit

The chorus sings of God's omnipresence

But all I can think about is my love

Trace the grain of wood, and feel His presence

And I finally look to God above

God forgives the zinnia for carelessness

Zinnia petals He forever will bless

Honeysuckle and Wisteria

The honeysuckle twines as life goes on
The wisteria weaves as days pass by
They take notice as their bored world does yawn
Their flowers float as one when wind does sigh
We climb together in the bonds of love
Of beauty, you meet the criteria
Hysteria crazy, but sane is love
I gladly welcome my wisteria
Your purple flowers mix with my yellow
Playful, you pretend to be hard to get
Your feelings about me are not mellow
Listen to my heart—blooming love will let
Loving honeysuckle willing to wait
Wisteria knows love cannot be late

Pansy and Petunia

The pansy and petunia fell in love
Because merriment occupies my thought
And hearts and ecstasy will stare above
And smiling Romance giggles when you sought
A body to feel, a body to touch
Because your presence is now haunting me
Said petunia to pansy about such
And the pansy replied the same to me
We are pansies and petunias to be
Because I knew in an instant that you
Were love at first sight, a pansy to be
Search for symbolic sensation in you
But you respond to me with a question:
"Waitress, have you any a suggestion?"

Iris

I have faith in this love that it will last

An iris flower in the garden true

A feeling like this never in the past

My emotions I had to tell to you:

I have bravery to commit to him

But do I have courage enough to speak?

Love makes no sense, and love comes as a whim

I approach him, my voice shaky and weak

I have wisdom in understanding him

I made a pitiful first impression

But iris flower beautiful to him

Hormones: a lewd, eagerly obsession

And within him, he now has compassion

And he now has to take lustful action

Tulips

Here I am running through Spring to greet you
Flower field of tulips, every color
Me staring, giggling, and smiling at you
Because purple tulips the best color
The purple romance of our love takes on
The form of a tulip flower in spring
We return after some seasons are gone
And hope and happiness we always bring
We come to an elm tree and sit on roots
And tulips as far as the eye can see
Humbly spirited, trace bark grooves on roots
Because, when young, there is so much to be!
And tulips show the truth of spring season
And elm roots show love is without reason

Tropical Coconut's Love with Communication

I cannot help I have an ugly voice

I cannot help I am not perfect, but

My miserable flaws are not a choice

Water from the tropical coconut

Is musical and refreshing after

Dehydration and tiring, painful hate

We find common ground and singing laughter

And your love for me, you cannot berate

Though there will be a rain after sunshine,

The coconut never gives up sweet hope

Because happiness is a sign benign

And remember to talk and never mope

Rain invigorates coconut and tree

And we can find the sunshine when carefree

SECTION THREE

Problems with Devotion

Content Magnolia

Sacrificing pride feels like an insult
You could never find happiness within
Admit all of your sins; it is all your fault
Nature the magnolia is within
She never wants to be the way you are
Pious, before bed always will she pray
Nature the magnolia finds afar
Ruin her purity, rip her away!
I am finding it hard to forgive you
Never blame his sins upon another
Listening to my words, never will you
Never blame virtues upon another
Forget my words, fight elegant beauty
Ending it, all is none of your duty

July Diary

In July, I write my own diary
Roses grow in the field and die in blood
From white to red—no purity I see
Writing about flowers, take not a bud
I will go back to Spring within my mind
Missing the forsythia, write anew
Within the poetry, beauty I find
The forsythia will always love you
One needs to be devoted to her man
The rose cheats and has affairs with others
The forsythia only sees one man
She stays true to herself; yellow covers
The forsythia remains beautiful
And the withered rose should be dutiful

Eventually Return to Me, Will You?

We are who we are; we love who we love

Arabian dreams; Iranian sleep

The highest note my voice will go above

Within my mind, his luxury, I keep

Full of angst, upon the sleeper, comes he

My poetry is about the journey

The songs I sing are about his beauty

Tempted, he touches the dreamer, not me

Won't you stay? Don't I give you what you need?

The land fertile with jewels, and yet I weep

There faithful men in the poetry I read

Yet I do not care; my love falls too deep

When you are tired of her bed, come to mine

Beautiful lyrics, I'm a jewel divine

Art on the Walls

Kissing and cussing, but I can tell you
Silly stares, and insanely I love you
Touch me, I desperately want you to do
But beforehand, the truth I want from you
I look around at the art on the wall
Ugly to me, but meaningful to you
Too much within me, dizzy, I will fall
And happiness will always favor you
You love another; a woman can tell
To forget, to forgive: I cannot feign
My mind loud, the truth continues to yell
You sit quiet; I stand in mental pain
You sit there in guilt over your affair
Cry as, at the art on the walls, you stare

Petals in the Wind

Love singing in the air again today

The apple tree petals float in the wind

Belly full of laughter, never dismay

Because to him, love letters I will send

Of him, about him; always on my mind

Charming, enchanting, suave ... but delicate

Following fate and I always will find

Apple tree petals and I lose my wit

Because he will abandon me, I fear

To him, love like an apple tree petal

Individual lust is never dear

Separate from trees and never settle:

And I wish I never let him near me

Alone with the seasons I would not be

Affair in Fall

Joys of the world blow away with flowers
All the primroses could not have saved them
Because from the truth, he always cowers
Artificial and fake, roses of prim
I look to lavender to show the truth
He lacks love, devotion, and purity
Discovering with my internal sleuth
Because my happiness can never be
Emotional love fading like lilacs
And the lavender is done telling me
Mourning grief, and I need strength from lilacs
But no sweet perfume, and no sight to see!
Flower petals are rotting in the dirt
Affair in fall a painful, blooming hurt

Willow Tree in Wind

Feel sorrow like a willow tree in wind
Bending branches break, splintering away
Beauty, my watchful eyes try to defend
Totally dark is the new nightfall day
Dangerous desire—love—without a warning
No self-control to confuse what is real
Sigmund Freud's ideas were discerning
And I think jealousy's life, I will steal
Empty with no expression on my face
Because bloody lacerations create
And once and for all, I will kill his ways
Disloyalty, adultery, I hate
For actions of infidelity, he
Will regret his secret beknown to me

SECTION FOUR

Death as the Muse

Lose Control

I lose control with too much around me

I identify, but I am not it

The wind in the Willows whispers to me

Intelligent trees tell me I lack wit

Confess you want to leave me here alone

What have I become? Feelings disappear

Between the branches, past sunlight has shone

I don't need you to show me what I fear

All I love I know leaves me in the end

The familiar feeling, I remember

You betrayed me; myself I can't defend

Climbing trees, your sorrow I remember

I let you down; I see as I fall off

Trace your fingers along the bark so soft

Regret's Rhythm

For as long as I care to remember
Hatred has been allowed to breathe alive
Learning to love, teaching will remember
Listening to shame, feelings won't revive
I hold my breath, heart pounding with regret
Ignore the fluttering rhythm, I can't
Paying attention and memories fret
I'm answering nothing while questions rant
Knowledge gone, here I am, left in silence
My voice is echoless, never speaking
Hearing hatred's words, my mind's death intense
Heads thinking aloud, replies are shrieking
With life's decay, self-disgust buries me
Cold hands on your warm chest, rot beauty sees

A Frail Rose

Inside your loving eyes, I see passion

The thoughts of you kissing me makes me flirt

To create cruelty lacking compassion

You get rewarded after getting hurt

With sorrow pacing, inside me, I feel

I will always be alone and afraid

Blood and bruises beating me; it's not real

Failing to awake, forever I fade

Beauty dying in my bones, left to rot

Evil lies above, reading my tombstone

Searching for any sign, flowers were brought

My corpse decays away as the sun shone

As long as there are tears, there will be hope

Blooming again, we will all learn to cope

Hoarding the Decay

Internal conversations attack me

I remember that I can see your face

I had a dream that you dreamed about me

I look away so you can't see my face

I cannot ever look you in the eye

Ignoring the desperation, I live

In love, my heart will breathe a silent lie

Intense screaming, my pounding heart will give

Its phantasma fantasizes death's rest

Insane I'm called for keeping the decay

I cry as I feel your quiet, cold chest

I'm sorry, but there is nothing to say

You never wanted me to be this way

You will rot in my arms, sorrow to stay

Chloe's Tree

Autumn wind and winter sky above me
A shock of life, your excitement gave you
You are buried beneath the apple tree
Fruit never to be as the blossoms blew
As I kiss the ground, baffled I remain
Loss in the ashes, I'm sorry for you
Insist and persist: love is not in vain
Always consequences we never knew
Eat away at the sweet apple of time
Be immortal in your eternal rest
Branches swaying above, upward you climb
Heartbroken, missing you, memories blessed
In our hearts never to decay and rot
Emotions pestering as tears I fought

Defend Your Memory

With love, I will defend your memory
I will plant sunflowers by your tombstone
I will visit each day with a story
A story always with a happy tone
You were my guardian angel before
You were the person I would look to find
Laughter, and your memory I adore
Sunflowers in my hair, thoughts in your mind
I will ensure my promises I keep
I will ensure your legacy lives on
I will ensure not in vain tears I weep
Because your body forever is gone
In me, you have to live on in some way
Sunflowers comforting and ... you will stay

Sadness in Summer and Warmth in Winter

Sadness in summer and warmth in winter

All that I have ever wanted was you

I feel complete when my twin flame is here

But sadly, you are no longer around

And I feel your presence by the river

I want you—you haunt my being at day

And I remember the time you did drown

I will save you from the wrath of water

I will follow your voice to your dwelling

And I will fulfill my crazy promise

I have it in mind for all the seasons

Every breath I take, my heart pines for you

I lost myself in the river that day

I intend finding flames begetting me

Dirty Stench

Feeling alone, but worship another
Wallowing in misery, disgust came
Callous death inside the womb and mother
Of myself, I constantly feel shrill shame
Resting on the willow's roots do I weep
By willows at the pond, I always cry
Leap into water, your feelings I keep
Your despair and darkness would ask me why
I observe that I'm like a Lilypad
I hold the beauty, but I am not it
With postpartum depression, I am sad
Withdraw from lily flowers, wish for wit
I tell myself I am never alone
Miscarriage and morose heartbreak bemoan

Makeshift World

I rest my mind by the old ginkgo tree
The twigs are a wife to the lovely leaves
Fall floats within; widows they are to be
Fluttering onto ground, the trunk deceives
The air blows, and a gift lands on my lap
Dozing off dreamily, I sense feeling
Within my memory, there is a gap
Dying with disease, the bark is peeling
With old age comes a sacrifice of life
Tearing it down, it is a barren hole
My wooden heart, I sculpt with sorrow's knife
Branches intertwining, we were one soul
Daydreaming, my mind is brave to wonder
My makeshift world taught me not to ponder

Willing Weeds

With weeds waiting, death dwells while flowers fade

Danger approaches, color gravely scared

The hydrangea hides, protected by shade

To defy death, graceful vibrancy dared

Evil stomps on the blooms, digging up roots

Burying memories, dark blackening

Weeds choke hydrangeas, think of attributes

Tearful ruin and disgraceful sinning

And tearful regret and mournful remorse

Catastrophe grins, proud of disaster

Indeed, the sun kills the remains, of course

If death perishes, buds would grow faster

The earth has settled upon a cycle

Vicious or not, nutrients recycle

Poppy Petals

And where did life go, and when did death stay?
Anger in life and such sadness in death
Leave a poppy bouquet on graves, I may
For corpses of coffins, a heartfelt wreath
Aware of lifeless words reaching my ears:
"Decay echoes throughout my dead body
Inspiration decomposes with tears
But I am grateful for the grand poppy
And I admire beauty's wild-born flower."
And *I* listen to tension in the moans
And stare silent at a poppy flower
Because empathy understands his groans
And orange poppy petals are hopeful
That my happy deeds are never woeful

So As Souls Can See

The sick sweet taste lingers within my mouth

Adoring love fades to irritated

Kissing lips cuss in the beautiful south

The sound of your screams, annoyance hated

Repulsion makes artificial flowers

Reality's glory will be gorgeous

Your alive blue beauty never cowers

The firsts to wither continues to fuss

Why does it always have to be this way?

The sun gladly shines to melt fake designs

Happy hymns humming, sing sad souls away

But floating down, the wilted petal whines

Confusion must love what was meant to be

Let the flower fields grow so souls can see

Little Lotus Flower

Forget about the past, and come find me
The little lotus still has love for you
Flowers surrounding all around, you see
Indeed, overwhelming shame within you
Because you do not recognize me here
So come search for me; come reach for me now!
I promise you close by, and I am near
I remember your lovely wedding vow
Contemplate location, listen to sound
Do I search for you? Do I reach for you?
A rotting corpse to see my heart will pound
Sweating with nightmares because I miss you:
A widow this flower forever is
Lotus for graves; mossy tombstone I kiss

Camellias

Gratitude gracious; paradise petty

Because find the beauty in the ugly

And you do not trust my face—too pretty

But, please, will not you take a chance on me?

Intellectual logic, I favor

The world does not follow your willful ways

And I hope your love will never waver

Or I hope you cherish me anyway

A white camellia I am for now

So, reach out; try your emotions again

You may find faithful preferences allow

Heart within your chest, but still it has been:

Yet you are forever alive to me

And disgusting rot is beauty I see

SECTION FIVE

Star-Crossed

Lovers;

Unhealthy

Love

Frustrated Fall

Chaos everywhere, there is never time
I will hope for an Indian Summer
Feeling the heat, the vine will always climb
Wisteria, a welcome newcomer
Ungrateful, regret with frustrated fall
Bad impression, ginkgo leaves in the dirt
No wisteria growing beauty tall
Head full of doubt, attention, I divert
Cold wind blowing on the flower petals
Cowardly trees will start to lose their leaves
Landing on my lap, a ginkgo leaf falls
No doubt, an Indian Summer believes
Fearful of change, I will look to the sky
Star-crossed lovers will always say good-bye

The Yellow Sundress

Dancing with the stars and the pale moonlight
Kissing me before you go as I cry
Looking at me dazed, and your smile shines bright
Please, understand before we say good-bye:
Yellow, a romantic color in me
There can be beauty even with weakness
Daring red lipstick is the fierce to be
Avoid sinning and you will find your bliss
I found you; a glutton for love, I am
The lust I feel has to be avoided
A Southern woman I forever am
Everybody hurts; one day, we are dead
Someday this pain will find use within you
But in the end, it won't matter for you

Elm of Sorrow

After being cut, elm trees grow again
I would keep myself; I would find a way
Full of sorrow, yourself you have not been
Even with time, pain does not go away
Around the elm tree branches, ivy curls
And grows—no longer any room for me
Love not appearing, but hateful fury
With you: a happy heart is not to be
You could have it all, but I let you down
Focus on the pain to kill what I hurt
When I am laughing, you happen to frown
Leaving me, you do dig me out of dirt
Ivy covers; the sun can't warm my face
We separate, yet nothing takes your place

Crying Pigeons

There are nature's flowers with purple dye
Other shades left for the mansion of Prince
Flinching, cringing, at the sound of doves' cry
Me of your love, your words cannot convince
Come to the garden gate bearing a gift
Anxiety! My beating heart will pause
A vicious cycle! You—you, with your gift!
Never satisfied, staring at your flaws
The heart is between the sky and the dirt
Unhappiness will make still pounding hearts
Meaningful mistakes ever on alert
Because cruelty will unite bleeding hearts
I watch the pigeon's wings glide through the air
No cries to be heard; I ignore your glare

I Hope Your World Is Kind

Yelling at me are the colors' tulips
Looking at the ground, I ignore the dirt
With the feeling of flowers on my lips
The thought of you kissing me makes me flirt
Sometimes I think you want me to touch you
Here I am, running through spring to meet you
Will you look for me as I look for you?
With anger always, how could I love you?
No passion within the season of love
Timid, I flinch as I watch you approach
Hating my heart, you, I am afraid of
Loud my heart beats as you tenderly touch
Beautiful tulips are fading away
Nothing but your scarred stem was left to stay

Forgotten Songs

Some that are breathing do not deserve life
Remember lyrics from forgotten songs
Seasons change, and the peace starts to form strife
Leaving your memory, I won't be long
I will come back and sing inside your mind
The turntable spins the record again
Dizzy and blurry, my voice you will find
Next to me, and duets, we will sing in
And I'll wait for you, and I'll be the same
Silently crying, harmonize love's fate
You see my smile, sweet melodies with shame
Loving me forever, heart filled with hate
But you'll be the same, and I will not wait
When you want to change, it will be too late

Paranoid Plum

No comfort can stop these tears from falling
He can't even cry; he won't even sigh!
My feelings bruised purple, you are calling
Overripe plums on ground, trees scream good-bye
Paranoid, the fruit says "Hello" to dirt,
"My time with the branches ended so soon."
Punched by sorrow, faces forever hurt
Blossoms regret their beauty's painful bloom
I want to taste delicious youth again
Does anyone feel the same way as me?
Comforted by the thought of you and sin
Unsure when any angel's death I see
I want to go back to the way we were
Colored by you, the plum's flesh always sore

Blank Is Our Rotting Gaze

Quiet, rest in your unvisited tomb
You lived faithfully a hidden feeling
We used to be so close, but we faced doom
Looking down at loss and corpses kneeling
And tears will fall looking up at the sky
I wish life will bring back our dead embrace
Like every star-crossed lover, say good-bye
Never meant to be, we go decay's pace
Hearts slow down with the glistening above
I'll do anything to take back my tears
Black but bright: nights transform beautiful love
Lonely forever, weep and scream with fear
Destiny and stars against us always
Seeing nothing, blank is our rotting gaze

Passion Is Shattered Glass

I will show him he has not broken me
I will not break the mirror of duty
Passion's shattered glass has wisdom bloody
And intelligence is within beauty
War within, I hide the scars of my past
In the memories of darkness afresh
My rational intuition will last
But sorrow is cutting into my flesh
I will show him what he can't ever see!
I will tell him what his ears cannot hear!
I will tell him in love I cannot be!
I will show him how he is to me dear!
Arteries rip away with rotting hearts
Closed veins open up sadness if he parts

Weeping Like a Willow

Within the wild wood is wacky wanting
The willow wished for the weigela
But just like a willow and weigela
We were the weak whimpering of a warning

The wind of wicked wonders won't teach warmth
The whispers of the worthless are wintry
The wealthy wash of the wildflower
Wasted to the white of a woodruff

I withdrew wishes of your welcoming
Woe is me when the waltz of worship waned
Wronged, you waged war on the winged worth I wallowed in
With the whip, my will has whittled away

Winter walks within, and your wonder has wilt
My woebegone wheeze woke with a wail
I whine as my warmth's wind winks with the wreckage
My soul wavers worthless and weary

One's wit of a willow and weigela
Is whimsy in the wimpy weakness of wooing
They won't weave like a wisteria
A wall is a waste with the wish of a window

Waiting a while saves the wiping of worries
Webbing with the weather wrecked the wielding of wanting

Brief Butterbean

You were a beautiful blackthorn branch
I saw benefits of this bargain
Baggy and bad, you were too big for this box
But blind and bewitched, I wasn't bothered

It felt like being a bisected butterfly
The bulbs began in full bloom:
The buttercup beamed without the baggage
The belladonna blazed by no bulk

Being backstabbed wasn't bearable
I was blue like a bellflower
And my blush bleached to baby's breath
You buried and befell my bliss

You bred no balance and betrayed the barrier
But this bewildered butterfly is be-winged
I will burst a bolt out of this blustery breeze
I am bailing out and will bandage the broken barriers

My bona fide beauty has biting, bold backbone
Bye, I banter; you're beyond barren of blessings

Dahlias and Violets

Dignity and powerful pride within
Dahlia flowers an annual plant
Committed bonds form and passion has been
Embarrassed elegance will vent and rant
And the violet flower hears with heart
Always listens, always accepts and cares
Soon the forming of love will have to start
Purple flowers have soft petals and stares
And violets always faithful and true
And dahlias thorough, appreciative
Violet questions what dahlia knew
Because love will take the initiative
Dahlias and arrogance are the same
Love not lasting, violets not to blame

SECTION SIX

Loneliness

The Oak and Aspen

Transcend the lies and look into my eyes

To protect your image, you tell falsehoods

Feeling nothing and you ignore my cries

Escaping you, I ran into the woods

The ripe acorns on the ground hurt my feet

Wind in the hardwood trees whispers to me

Hearing nothing, I beg it to repeat

Dropping more acorns, the oak glares at me

No one pretends to love my company

Until I see the sequins on aspens

Staring with wonder, the leaves impress me

Laughing at emotions are the aspens

I left you only to find more cruelty

Tears stain my face; alone I am to be!

Laughter's Wrinkle

I comprehend that I am just a girl
But can I change lives? I don't think I can
Bored, I look at the stars above the world
Hold me accountable; I need a man
Not wanting to think Earth as part of space
I sit quietly with an empty heart
Money for the space race, I touch your face
We can't eat money; power has no heart
I am nothing as I repeat myself
Sit underneath the stars, your eyes twinkle
Hearing your laughs, me alone with myself
Smiling with my eyes, I fear a wrinkle
Paranoia paralyzes my mind
Causing me distress, love I cannot find

The Drunk Artist

The tongue wastes precious words; the pen frees them

Finally, I can see for myself truth

My thoughts are straining to see not of him

I cannot help it—however uncouth

Rhododendron wishes it all away

The message of warning—always resent

More flowers blooming, more sunlight at day

To harm me, I have determined he meant

The random red rhododendron is rare

Poetry written, and poetry gone

At cruel misery I will cuss and swear

My emotions decay, and I am done

Found crying by the rhododendron bush

I hush my mouth and become a drunk lush

Heart of an Iris

Ignoring the sun, the yellow remains
Unaware that we have or that we know
Purple romance flattering, love disdains
Growing in beauty without sunlight's glow
Recently sorrow is awakening
But the iris stands still with a bold heart
Looking to the sky, gleefully taking
Through love and pain, the petals never part
No flower withering or held to me
I wish to be the heart of an iris
Freeing my bravery never to be
Face certainty, and lips hope for a kiss
Dying to catch my breath, why don't I learn?
My desperation forever to yearn

Withering Roses and Wants

You need to enter your soul's feeling mind
Breathe as hearts travel through a flower field
Roses here, and with beauty, you are blind
Strolling beside in insanity's field
Perfect no longer, there are painful flaws
With unwanted white, I paint roses red
Impure, undaunted; audience applause
Change of color, and memories had bled
And hatred blocks the sun, flowers falter
Because love is turning into hatred
And calamities when now I palter
Vague, ambiguous doubt with roses red
I'd rather be with a friend in the dark
Then be walking alone with light's warm mark

Handsome and High

High as the sun, I might shine upon you
No one will care when the world has gone mad
And you can ignore what you thought you knew
Because scandalous wisdom will feel sad
And I want you to feel blinded by light
Look indirectly, but don't look away
Dancing with Mary Jane always feels right
To my happiness, I will find my way
The sun was a mother to Mary Jane
I feel not ashamed of my handsome high
Humorous and blurry, feelings insane
And my love I will have to verify
Now I get high to get you off my mind
But it reminds of when memories shined

Words Die

I refuse to repeat what I have said
Intelligent conversations never
Heard not by you, but tears I will not shed
I don't mean to interrupt you ever
Hidden sorrow, no satisfaction true
And disagreeing arguments of woe
Secret emotions will never hate you
But feel anger with frustration I know
When sadness within rage, I speak of joy
Because of you, I have become jaded
Misunderstood dying love will annoy
My eyes cry out blood as my heart faded
I pretend to believe in simple thoughts
In words' tomb, my soul forever will rot

Thoughts Have No Constraints

Decorating crown, Baby's Breath in hair
Endearment will shatter the glass of hate
However handsome a complexion fair
On his wedding day and my horror late
And he left me at the altar today
Embarrassment withering Baby's Breath
Flowers will wilt as my heart feels dismay
Screaming with nightmares and sorrowful death
My wounds return to me when I awake
My heart torn open, throbbing love does ache
Blood covering and crying no mistake
Because the truth of love one cannot fake
Mutilated discussions, cruel complaints
Apologize as thoughts have no constraints

Alone and Lonely

The wisteria climbs across the door
Its light lilac flowers are draping down
I've pushed others away I can't ignore!
I am sorry my petals are not brown
By mistake a weed I am thought to be
Please, do not dig me up with abhorrence!
Please, give me a color and scent to be
Please, give me a chance, give me tolerance
And summer citrus I want to be like
I want orange blossoms to decorate
Lilac purple no longer: this you like
And happy orange blossoms weave the gate
I wreaked havoc and consequence on hearts
Me no longer, only pieces and parts

Passionate Prayer

Insomnia lies to awaken me
Regret hangs heavy in my sleepy eyes
Wont with passionate prayers whispered by me
Soulful secret, sorrowful spirit sighs
He was there when I needed him the most
My only wish is that he will return
I held his hands and kissed his lips, I boast
I will never again be of concern
Because bashful feelings exist in me
And I fell ruthlessly in love with him
Bedlam's anarchy within heartfelt me
And I lack intellect when around him
Civility gone; touches I cherish
Unwilfully alone, pray and perish

Doomed Dogwood

There are two sides to any a story
Daydreaming, but look up at the bare tree
Digging up the dogwood, words are stormy
In the light of Christmas morning, I see
The past read about bravery, I know
Silently, I observe the real meaning
The dogwood's courage makes a true hero
And seemingly the sun rays are beaming
Decaying without decoration's pride
Wish to die with flowers, snow a cold doom
So, this is Christmas, and your tongue has lied
The dogwood fades away, ash in a tomb
Beauty has honor, snowflakes a sentence
Because heavy hearts have no admittance

Cactus Flower

Waiting for you is like waiting for rain
But the love in cactus flowers endures
Because happiness never feels disdain
And I lip synch and listen to The Cure
Because I am willing to wait for you
And I will need a love song to woo you
I learn about life you already knew
I feel emotions you already do
But a cactus flower never gives up
So I am surreal while in solitude
I will look to the sky; I will look up
Rain without you, I change my attitude
No understanding and no connection
Flowing to my mind is no conception

Forget-Me-Nots

Strangers' sorrowful words can derange you

I think of who you were before she came

I remember your laugh when I think of you

She changed you, and now you are not the same

And I was always mad in love with you

Although you never would take heed of me

And I was always riant around you

Although you would never look and see me

My tear-stained heart fills with forget-me-nots

As forget-me-nots I send to lush love

Because you sit silent as your soul rots

Please, I need you to feel again and love!

You were once the only sane person and …

… Now never notice when I hold your hand

Clematis Purple Along the Graveyard Fence

Everything has been wrong since you have died

Clematis grows along the graveyard fence

Rust and peeling paint, I cannot abide

Flowers' purple a color too intense

Because black is the color of sorrow

Shadows, a mystery not beautiful

Fingertips and metal fence: scent I know

Standoffish tears fall at your funeral

And I wish you had a diamond tombstone

Because granite never enough for you

With grief, time stands still as I sob and moan

Your perspective would think hope's flowers true

I do not want to use my heart again

Lonely here, you buried there: pride hidden

SECTION SEVEN

With or Without Regret

California and Irrigation

Make an impression on me and pardon
Style wholistic, I offer no advice
Love unhappy; flowers in the garden
Cruel virtues repeat, oceans deep with vice
Fear is tomorrow like salt in the rain
With tears flowers wither and die away
Life crying ocean's saltwater in vain
Light dreams in red comes the sunrise of day
Words mix with salt, and water flows the mind
Laughter evil, ocean deep and unknown
Flowers in the garden, I cannot find
Feeling the fright of love no seed has grown
Let me tell you the story of water
Oceans traveling and flowers falter

The Lightbulb Flickers

I look around me to find I am lost
The lightbulb flickers for days upon days
I am always cold, but there is no frost
To solve my problems, there are woeful ways
Alcohol warms me up to cool me down
A lightweight I am, and drunk I will be
If I am happy, I smile, but I frown
I want them all to get away from me
There is snow in my heart, sun in the sky
I need to find my way, but I cannot
I am a failure, but I know not why
I needed a drink, and a drink I sought
The lightbulb flickers for days upon days
Alcohol within, but sober in ways

Paradox

My fingers are crooked, but they are strong
A flower will wither, but still will be
The truth from a person's lips can be wrong
My memory's image I cannot see
But who am I to describe life to you?
I am a philosopher of flowers
I cannot ever tell you what to do
In my dreams, I run through fields of flowers
That is forever a lie, I do fear
I awaken in the night from myself
Minds left yelling, yelling loudness I hear
And I cannot ever correct myself
I cannot sit still, and I cannot sleep
But my emotions I will always keep

Bigger Than Me

Inspiration I need to find for me

For me, I cannot now pretend to wait

Idle with my boredom, I cannot be

My haunting ignorance, I cannot hate

It's like you have a chance in a lifetime

But your one shot becomes bigger than you

Music blasting, I listen to the rhyme

And I know now I am unlike to you

I do not understand why you do this

Stamping and dancing, but you touch my hair

You do not understand why I am this

And into the distance, I have to stare

I am overstimulated and cold

Sweating with anxiety, wording bold

Beautiful Breeze

Like summer's warm breeze, you entered my life
Wind carries the smell of flower's beauty
Withstanding the blows, the dogwood has strife
Peace within nature, love keeps its duty
The sun sets, and darkness covers the earth
Nothing dims the light that comes from within
Heart beating in dirt for the spirit's birth
The fragile tree waits for the cold to end
We watch the sun rising, your hand in mine
We touch the bark, resting beneath dogwoods
Looking at branches, your feelings I pine
The grown petals in Spring are blooming buds
Forgive me for becoming who I feign
Time destroying, beauty's head never sane

Selfishly Sensing

The world's beauty was shielded from my eyes
The pleasures of this world are quite blurry
Losing enchanting charm, his glamour dies
None left for me as he feels luxury
Wails of pain, and he will be around me
Giving me hope, a butterfly does sigh
Ripping off wings so they're now not to be
Cacophonous caterpillars will die
And stumbling through a flower field, I feel
All of the petals I tear off with hate
A gorgeous lie, their glory is not real
And beauty will smell the sincere too late
Surrounding wrongs that we cannot endure
And life's luscious injustice without cure

Poisonous Person

Unhappy prepare for playful presence
You penalize predicted pleasure's pride
Promised cruelty is your pouring essence
You take poetic pessimism's side
Pianos play, sing musical pieces
One must persuade the performer to dance
Persistent perfume's potential ceases
Popular passion is personal chance
Poppy petals petrify, pleasant prayer
Perseverance ponders precision now
Participation's prevalence does share
Pitiful patterns patiently allow
Pale positivity is paused by pests
Unpromising pain prevails in protests

Identity a Trap

When will the voice in my head escape me?
I feel my thoughts becoming who I am
Identity, a trap most cannot see
And prejudice thinks it knows who I am
Unaware I am ripping flesh away
Sticky, warm liquid covers my hands now
No one can notice when, silent, I pray
Dispose skin onto the floor I allow
No sympathy and don't look down on me
Supposed angels with no compassion
Demon within, the Devil is to be
I'm frustrated with my painful passion
Mindless words come out: I am chained to hate
Mortified Lucifer leaves Heaven's gate

Resented Reincarnation

In a state of dreaming, I am decay
If I die tonight, at least I will know
A peaceful butterfly I'll be at day
I'll come back resented to haunt you so
My reincarnated soul will be saved
Fluttering by, revisiting beauty
With flowers and disgrace, a sidewalk paved
Admiring flowers my loving duty
Flying, I will never leave you alone
You never honored the essence of me
See-through wings, but confessions never shone
The glory of life you never could see
Tormented, I rip off my precious wings
Shocking distress, and my hostile scream sings

Fuchsias

¡Debes pensar en otras personas!
But you are not me and never will be
Beautiful colors, petals of fuchsias
And you will look to the flower in me
Strangers my warm heart will gladly welcome
My colors attract hummingbirds above
Greedy, arrogant deviance will come
They take advantage, and this is not love!
Purple magenta crumpled and lifeless
And the bees pass by with their laughing jests
Harrowing and horrendous, not guiltless
Because hummingbirds and bees were my guests
Aggravated but gentle, I need change
Paradise waits and ruthless, I estrange

Deadheading Progress

And there I go, and here I am again
Echinacea looks for the light of day
But me, a difficult, drunk mess with gin
Because mournful angst came with me to stay
Admiration, a pale, romantic pink
Echinacea, a kind, rugged flower
But I pass out, unconscious when I blink
Echinacea is more than a flower
But a symbol of qualities to be
And a symbol of when I am again
And a symbol when grief reminded me
And a symbol of reasons I drink gin
Because resilience never in me
Deadhead the flower forever for me?

SECTION EIGHT

Acceptance

Shapeshifting Poetry

They say they will listen, but they will not

I wonder who all my words have gone to

And they say they can care, but they cannot

I feel my worries were wasted on you

If I had to be a man, I would cry

Cry because that is never who I am

Women empowered through beauty and I

Wish a gorgeous goddess I were and am

And I know I cannot write poetry

Poetry, yet, is a skill most possess

I ask myself: to be or not to be?

With drama and death, Shakespeare may obsess

That is forever who he was and is

But not me; shapeshifting poetry is

No Oaths of Betterment

Floating and frolicking when we were young
Handsome hands always reaching up my skirt
Love poems about bad breakups were sung
And with every man, I would always flirt
I had hated my appearance for years
Until I remembered my confidence
Stain my face never will your pretty tears
I have never even thought of you since
It is like a sick cycle of self-growth
And I can never get ahead of it
Cussing and drinking, never swear an oath
An oath will not make you better for it
Without drama, what is a love poem?
Flirting back at me, and I smile at him

Angelic Azalea

Enemies make us into who we are

Abused, and you are an abrasive man

Abstract adopted amaze is not far

Dream and sleep, into your mind's woods, you ran

Obstacles appear, you step on a twig

Shaking by aspens, adrenaline acts

Without a choice, you dance the Devil's jig

Pursuing you, your foe follows your tracks

You are accustomed to this addiction

With their appearance, you will aim away

You abandon heart in agitation

You should acknowledge the price you will pay

Admire azalea's angelic beauty

Tickled pink you are with your pure duty

Random Return

Repeatedly respect for rival rot
Reoccurring rage rushes to return
Reappear ruthless, raw regret will not
And I read your lips with thoughtful concern
I recognize I wronged you in my way
I realize I restrict sporadic love
You cannot grow when the sun looks away
Because rapturing pain remarks of love
And I am filled with only hate for you
Earthworms wriggle under rhododendrons
The belle and the nasty, no artists drew
Redeem in drought, but no rhododendron
Because you are the artist; I, the fraud
Refuse and chastise, but your wisdom broad

Shadows Within Us

You don't just breathe in; you also breathe out
Beautiful dreams mean nothing just to some
Enlightening shined, and I feel no doubt
Wishes and symbols, deepness will not come
Hypocrites cause me such anger and rage
Will connections bond? Answer no and yes
Shackled to the cave wall, always a cage
And empathy makes me feel more, not less
I meant it when I said we're like fruit flies
Judging others, we gnaw on rotting sweets
How does your brain think? Why does your soul sigh?
Disappointment, and victors feel defeat
There are cruel shadows within us always
To reach empty, dull minds, truth can find ways

Flowering Baby's Breath

Save yourself the trouble and walk away
Discovery and appreciation
You enjoy sniffing the fresh air of day
Fascist democracy in our nation
Chanting together, but I do not join
I will sit and stare at the Baby's Breath
Peaceful, simple: flower petals adjoin
You only sing music with thoughts of death
I am a sick person spreading sadness
Fingertips stroking, I turn petals brown
Hurting all I touch and full of madness
Dirt is filled with decay as I look down
I wish I would become who I am now
Baby's Breath growing, life flowers allow

Magnolia and Sweet Pea

I met you during a warm summer breeze
You were always within the world and me
Our hearts are magnolia and sweet peas
But natural closeness never to be
Once tame, now will grow wild in the rubble
Your perfect purity has dignity
Vulnerable and uncomfortable
And magnolia cynical of me
Sweet pea simple, and triumph would achieve
Magnolia in you, and calm of heart
We held delicate pleasure, I believe
In the same warm summer breeze, we depart
Sweet peas never linger on loss of love
Flower petals float in the wind above

Life Swims in a River

While the sun still shines and wild rivers flow
And the butterflies still flutter by me
And beauty's diversity flowers show
Your bottomless bravery is to be
When leaves do fall and decay on the ground
And returning wind blows your breath away
And nighttime will lengthen with darkness bound
Your bottomless bravery grows at day
When freezing snow provides dirt with rare warmth
And snowflakes provide a blanket as proof
And the solid river cannot move forth
Your bottomless bravery all will soothe
Life will swim on with all of the seasons
Your heart still beats with loving words' reasons

Touching Heaven's Sky

Slumber through the light of the winter sun
I feel so cold now that the warmth has gone
But this is Christmas, and what have you done?
Of nice, nostalgic feelings you have none
Snow covers the nest, and my heart freezes
I stop malicious control over me
Wistful sentimentality ceases
I learn how to fly, am finally free
I see festive Christmas tree lights aglow
Snowflakes flutter onto feathers and me
Touch heaven's sky—the bird in me will know
And excitement is soaring within me
Acquaintances with emancipation
Christmas had allured anticipation

SECTION NINE

Original Paintings

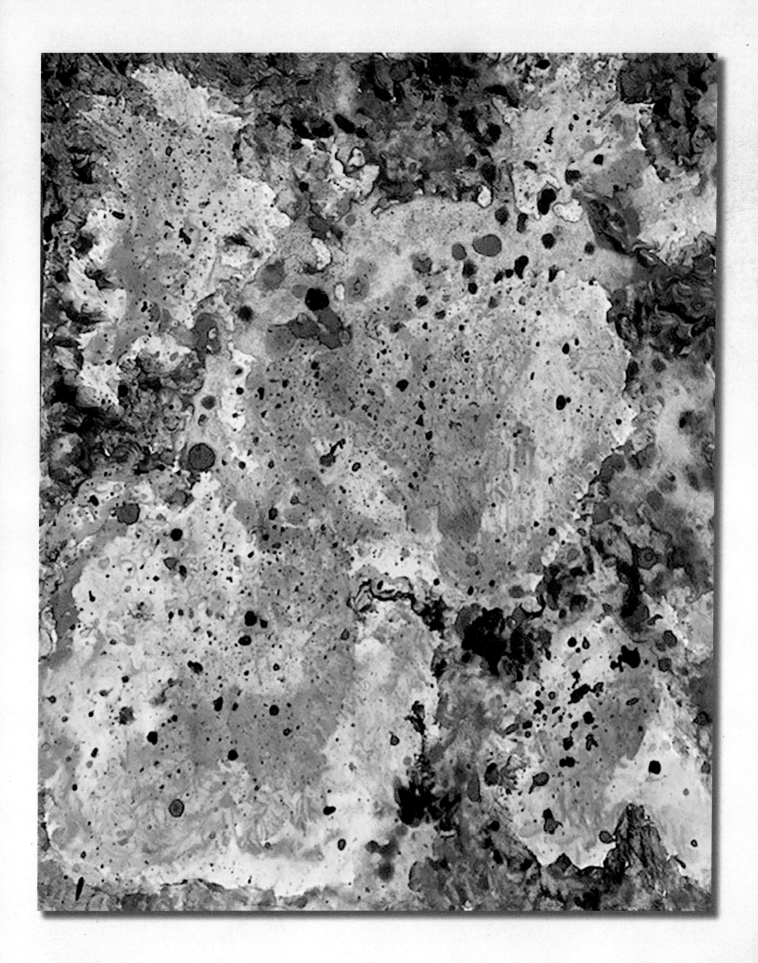

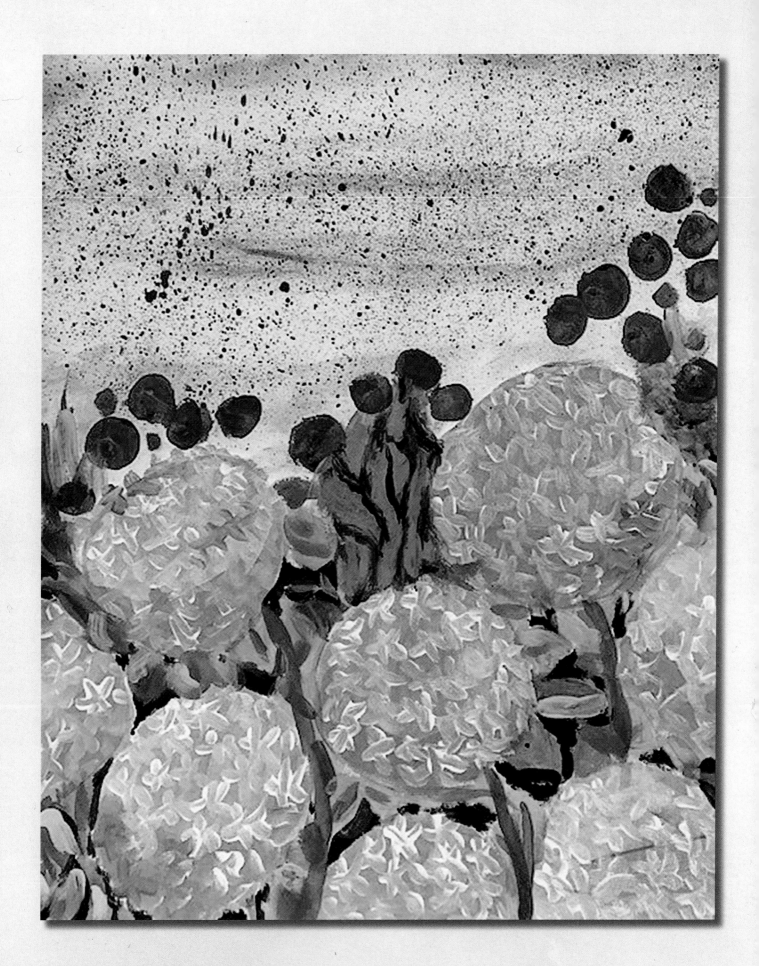

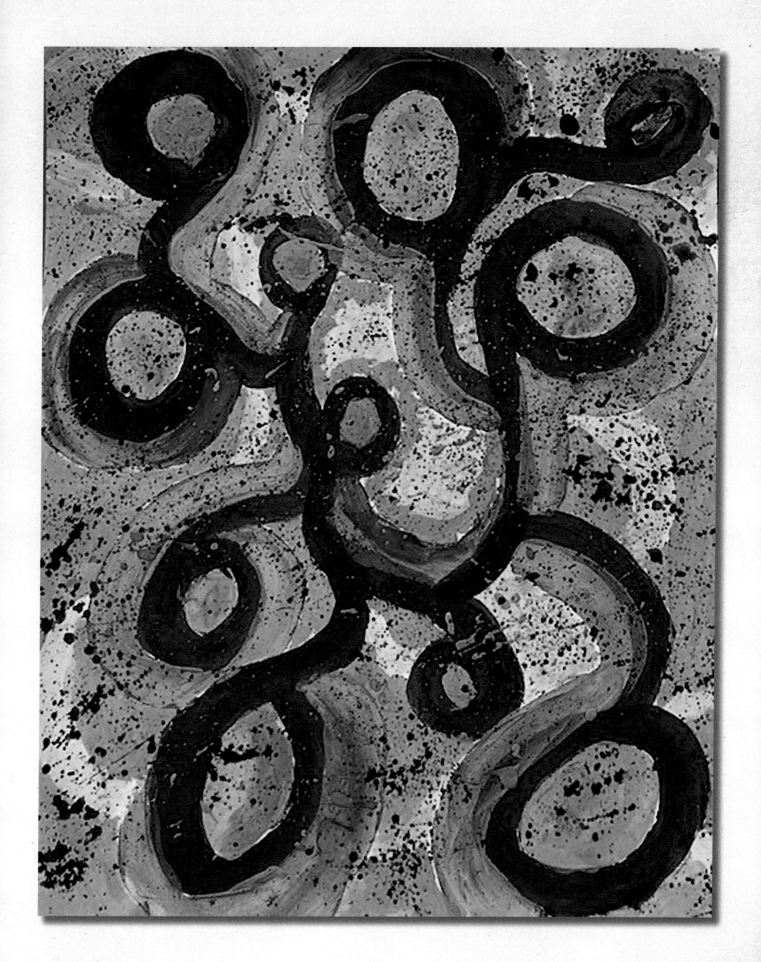

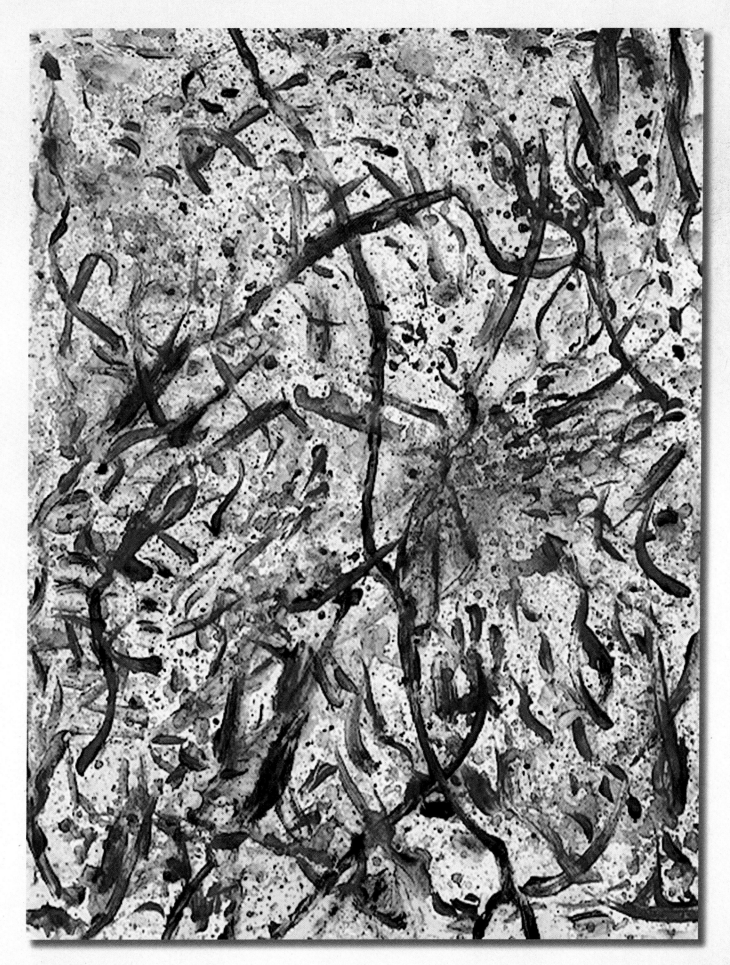

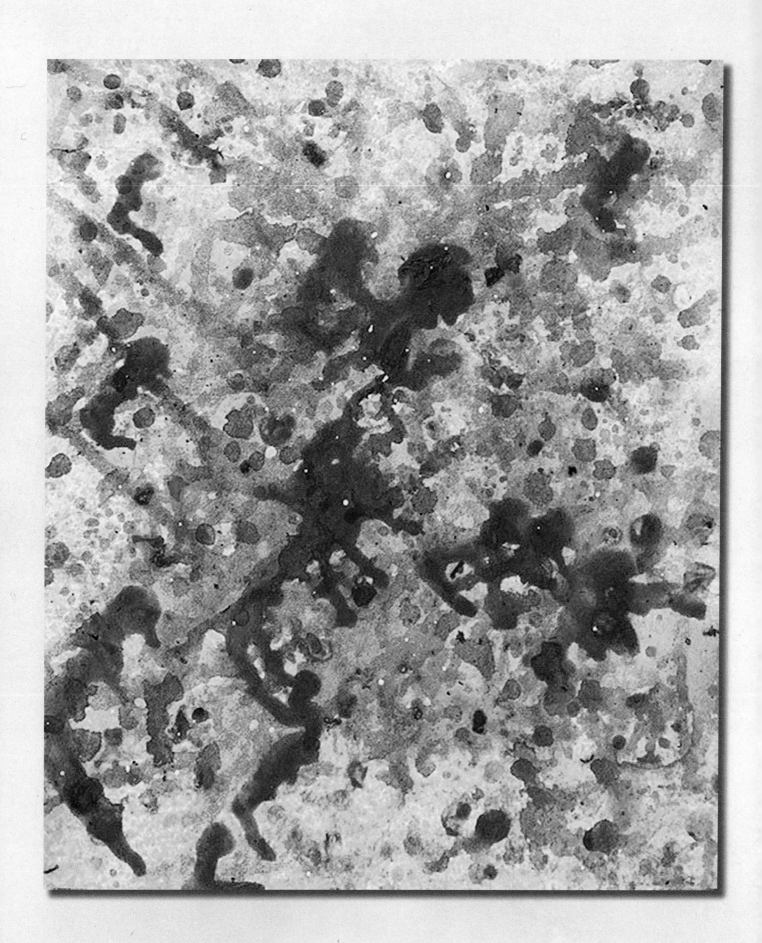

Index

L

Like summer's warm breeze, you entered my life 94

Lost in the darkness, I'll find you somewhere 25

Love singing in the air again today 40

M

Make mine moonlight, poets say to the sky 16

Most cannot think for their own selves ever 4

My fingers are crooked, but they are strong 92

N

No comfort can stop these tears from falling 66

P

The pansy and petunia fell in love 31

Q

Quiet, rest in your unvisited tomb 67

R

Repeatedly respect for rival rot 105

S

Sacrificing pride feels like an insult 36

Sadness in summer and warmth in winter 50

Save yourself the trouble and walk away 107

Showing me the truth, at least now I know 15

Sisters Cecilia and Lorelei 14

Slumber through the light of the winter sun 110

Soft and mellow, lighting up lively love 22

Some that are breathing do not deserve life 65

Starry-eyed Louisiana, you love 19

A storm stirring mud somewhere deep inside 27

Strangers' sorrowful words can derange you 86

Strawberries, sweet and juicy, soft and ripe 17

T

There are nature's flowers with purple dye 63

There are two sides to any a story 84

They say they will listen, but they will not 102

The tongue wastes precious words; the pen frees them 76

Twining toward each other, they tangle 11

U

The unforgiving feeling of doubt grows 26

Unhappy prepare for playful presence 96

W

Waiting for you is like waiting for rain 85

We are who we are; we love who we love 38

When I die, I do not want a casket 8

When will the voice in my head escape me? 97

While the sun still shines and wild rivers flow 109

The wisteria climbs across the door 82

With love, I will defend your memory 49

With sorrowful grief, this is my silence 2

With weeds waiting, death dwells while flowers fade 53

Within the wild wood is wacky wanting 69

The world's beauty was shielded from my eyes 95

Y

Yelling at me are the colors' tulips 64

You don't just breathe in; you also breathe out 106

You knew all along that it was not you 23

You need to enter your soul's feeling mind 78

You tell me I leave a void with despair 5

You were a beautiful blackthorn branch 70